KETTLEBELL TRAINING

The Ultimate Kettlebell Workout to Lose Weight and Get Ripped in 30 Days

By John Powers

Copyright© 2014 by John Powers – All rights reserved.

Copyright: No part of this publication may be reproduced without written permission from the author, except by a reviewer who may quote brief passages or reproduce illustrations in a review with appropriate credits; nor may any part of this book be reproduced, stored in a retrieval system, or transmitted in any form or by any means – electronic, mechanical, photocopying, recording, or other – without prior written permission of the copyright holder.

The trademarks are used without any consent, and the publication of the trademark is without permission or backing by the trademark owner. All trademarks and brands within this book are for clarifying purposes only and are owned by the owners themselves.

Disclaimer: The information within the book *Kettlebell Training – The Ultimate Kettlebell Workout to Lose Weight and Get Ripped in 30 Days* is intended as reference materials only and not as substitute for professional advice. Information contained herein is intended to give you the tools to make informed decisions about your body's physical level and ability to perform exercises. Every reasonable effort has been made to ensure that the material in this book is true, correct, complete, and appropriate at the time of writing.

The Author and Publisher has strived to be as accurate and complete as possible in the creation of this book, notwithstanding the fact that he does not warrant or represent at any time that the contents within are accurate due to the rapidly changing nature of the subject and the internet (third party website links). Nevertheless, the Author and Publisher assume no liability or responsibility for any omission or error, for damage or injury to you or other persons arising from the use of this material. Reliance upon information contained in this material is solely at the reader's own risk.

Any perceived slights of specific persons, peoples, or organizations are unintentional. This book is not intended as a substitute for the medical advice of physicians. Like any other sport, kettlebells poses some inherent risk. The Author and Publisher advise readers to take full responsibility for their safety and know their limits. It is also recommended that you consult with a qualified healthcare professional before beginning any training on the subject. Before practicing the skills described in this book, be sure that your equipment is well maintained, and do not take risks beyond your level of experience, aptitude, training, and comfort level.

First Printing, 2014 – Printed in the United States of America

*"If it doesn't CHALLENGE you
It doesn't CHANGE you"*

– *Fred DeVito*, co-founder of Exhale

TABLE OF CONTENTS

Introduction	1
Chapter 1 – What is Kettlebell Training?	3
History of the Kettlebell	4
Science Behind Kettlebell Training	7
Chapter 2 – Kettlebell Training is for Everyone	11
Functional Fitness Training	12
Kettlebell Training for Men	13
Kettlebell Training for Women	14
Adapting Kettlebell Training for Specific Needs	16
Chapter 3 – Kettlebell Training for Every Purpose	17
Cardio Workouts	18
Core Workouts	19
Cross Training	20
Legs and Lower Body	21
Strength	22
Toning and Shaping	23
Weight Loss	24
Physical Therapy and Rehabilitation	25
Chapter 4 – How to Choose the Right Kettlebell	27
Weight	28
Shape and Size	30
Materials and Finishes	32
Brands of Kettlebells	34
Chapter 5 – Kettlebell Style, Form and Technique	37
Style	38
Holds	40

Posture	43
Safety Tips	45
The Importance of Active Recovery	47
Chapter 6 – The Fundamentals of Kettlebell Exercises	49
Before You Begin	50
Understanding the Terms	58
Chapter 7 – 30 Basic Kettlebell Exercises and How to Perform Them	61
Grind Exercises	63
Ballistic Exercises	83
Chapter 8 – Kettlebell Workout Programs	95
Basic Workout	96
Simple Toning Workout	97
Easy to Modify Full-Body Workout	98
Kettlebell Workout for All-Over Strength	99
Killer Core Workout	100
Beyond the Basics	102
Muscle Building with Kettlebells	103
Kettlebell Workouts During Pregnancy	104
Chapter 9 – Nutrition for Weight Loss and Management	105
What a Body Needs for a Healthy Diet	106
Turning the Body into a 'Fine-Tuned-Machine'	107
Carbohydrates Play a Crucial-Role	108
Beyond Carbohydrates	111
Maintain Adequate Hydration	113
Detoxification is Not Just a Fad	114
Conclusion	115
About the Author	117

INTRODUCTION

Getting in shape is something we always promise ourselves to do but, somehow, never get around to. How about if there were a quick, fun, and relatively easy way to accomplish it, though?

With kettlebells, virtually **anyone** with any beginning level of fitness **can develop a more toned, flexible body while losing weight**. In as little as 30 days, it is possible to see results and not feel as though you are submitting yourself to torture!

Kettlebells, those funny looking pieces of equipment that may be collecting dust in the corner of a gym, **provide a dynamic full-body workout** that can give you great results in less time and with greater convenience than traditional exercise programs. There are two reasons for this.

Kettlebells create an off-balance resistance that forces the cooperation of more muscles and muscle groups to burn a lot more calories, and, most importantly, they are a lot of fun!

From what began as an activity to pass the time at farmer's markets in Russia, the use of kettlebells has spread to gyms and workout rooms around the world. Given a wide variety of weights officially measured in *'poods'* (roughly 16 pounds), people of all ages and physical conditions can add kettlebell exercises to any traditional workout routine or even physical therapy program.

Simple, gentle lifts and swings can turn into dynamic, ballistic moves that demand tremendous coordination, flexibility, and strength. With the mastery of the *deadlift* and *swing*, you are on your way to developing as wide a variety of exercises as you want in order to incorporate practically every muscle in your body. For this reason, kettlebell training has successfully been added to the workouts of professional and competitive athletes as well as body builders for increased power, explosive strength, and muscle toning.

Kettlebells are essentially easy to use, but as with any new exercise program, it is important to discuss your overall health and fitness with a medical professional first. Additionally, proper form is crucial to the success of kettlebell training so a session or two with a certified instructor is the best way to start.

The information contained in **this book is designed to provide you with the basic facts you need to get started on a 30-day plan to a better, fitter body and lower weight**. It is not intended as medical advice or to offer any guarantee. What it does, however, is motivate you to take the steps needed for improving your health and fitness, providing simple instructions for beginning a terrific new exercise regimen.

Happy kettlebelling!

CHAPTER 1 – WHAT IS KETTLEBELL TRAINING?

Kettlebell training was once associated with circus strongmen but has now become a standard tool for both men and women in the quest for total-body fitness and increased strength. Kettlebells are great for standard weight lifting workouts but have also been proven to be quite effective for cardio training and can be used in High Intensity Interval Training (HIIT) or physical therapy programs as well.

History of the Kettlebell

Evidence exists that kettlebells were used for competition in Ancient Greece.

Some people believe that kettlebells as exercise tools are derived from Scottish curling stones which were used for sport as early as the 1500s. More recently, however, kettlebells are mentioned in a Russian dictionary dating back to 1704 and are referred to as weights used to measure grain, produce, and other goods. It is believed that farmers and other fair and festival participants began lifting and swinging these weights to demonstrate strength, and the competitive sport of kettlebelling was born.

In terms of exercise and legitimate sport, *Dr. Vladislav Kraevsky* is credited as the developer of the use of kettlebells for strength and weight training. In 1885, a facility dedicated to weight training and systematic muscular development was opened in Russia based on the findings of Dr. Kraevsky who had searched throughout Russia and Europe to uncover as much information as possible about exercise practices and programs.

As evidence of the success of Kraevsky's program spread, the use of kettlebells increased around the world. A number of world famous 'strong men' have been pictured holding kettlebells. The advent of the Russian Revolution, WWI, and subsequent political considerations caused the relative isolation of kettlebell usage to Russia where the sport continued to grow, and the benefits of using kettlebells for exercise became more and more apparent.

With the opening of international borders at the end of the 20th century and the spread of sport competition around the world, **kettlebelling** as a sport **is recognized** today and overseen **by a number of different organizations** such as the:

- *American Kettlebell Club (AKC)* – founded in 2004. Has been transformed into multiple Kettlebell Clubs across America.

- *Canadian Kettlebell Sport Federation (CKSF)*

- *International Gira Sport Federation (IGSF)*

- *International Kettlebell & Fitness Federation (IKFF)*

- *International Union of Kettlebell Lifting (IUKL)*

- *World Kettlebell Club (WKC) – organized in the USA in 2006.*

- *World Kettlebell Sports Federation (WKC)*

Science Behind Kettlebell Training

Instead of training isolated muscles, **kettlebell training is a functional training activity**. That means that the moves and demands of daily life or common sports are copied with the exercises done with the kettlebell. *Lifting, pushing, pulling,* and *reaching* are all part of kettlebell activities.

Why are kettlebells better than other weight-training activities?

One advantage of kettlebells over dumbbells, barbells, and machines is the ***dynamic, ballistic nature of the moves***. You can work slowly or quickly with kettlebells to perform a wide range of movements that are either not possible with standard weights or would require many different machines.

The most significant benefit of kettlebells, though, is the ***demand for greater inter- and intramuscular coordination and kinesthetic awareness*** to remain stable during the exercise. In other words, many more muscles and joints are involved in each kettlebell movement, and the entire body becomes part of the workout. The core, hips, and other muscles involved in stabilizing the body are constantly working.

As an extension of your arm, the ***kettlebell adds*** not only weight but also ***a dynamic feature that requires effort to control***. The movements – momentum and centrifugal force – force you to constantly adjust in order to maintain your grip and keep the kettlebell doing what you want. The constantly changing center of mass creates what is considered an unstable environment that the body must react to, and this is what **promotes greater**

physical capabilities such as:

- Balance
- Flexibility
- Agility
- Strength
- Mobility
- Speed
- Posture
- Range of motion

Another benefit of the dynamic nature of kettlebell training is the ***improvement*** that can be made ***in cardiovascular health***. Instead of intense aerobics, kettlebell training can elevate heart rate and improve lung capacity and actually do it in less time.

By working the entire body and involving many more muscles than most other exercises, the body becomes more of a fat-burning machine, and the metabolism is elevated, even after the exercise session is over.

This ***improved fat loss*** is due to the '*afterburn*' or *EPOC* (excessive post-exercise oxygen consumption) *effect* and will be discussed further in Chapter 3 – Kettlebell Training for Every Purpose.

Essentially, **the benefits of kettlebell training** can be summed up in these statements:

- Improvement in functional strength and mobility
- Utilization of full-body movement and multidirectional forces
- Ability to achieve maximum heart rate and VO2max for improved metabolism and cardio health
- Protection of joints through low-impact and ballistic movements
- Maximization of core strength
- Creation of lean body mass – no bulking up
- Constant engagement of core and stabilizer muscles for better posture and relief of back pain
- Reduction in the risk of osteoarthritis in women

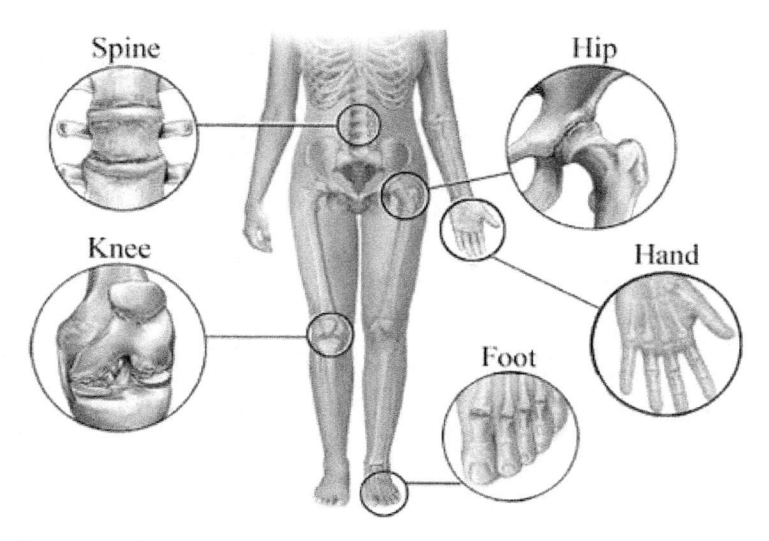

- Elevation of stress-relieving hormones and overall energy level
- Challenging workouts that can be changed easily to retain interest and keep you engaged
- Inexpensive and can be performed anywhere

CHAPTER 2 – KETTLEBELL TRAINING IS FOR EVERYONE

While most people look at kettlebells and wonder how in the world they can help them lose weight and get fit; once they give them a try, they are hooked. The reason that kettlebell workouts have become so popular is that they are quite simple and versatile, promote strength, endurance, and flexibility, and have tremendous potential for everyone.

People of all ages and fitness levels can easily get involved with kettlebell training. It is a great tool for all-around fitness and body shaping as well as weight loss and strength building. Posture is improved, and there are also plenty of cardio benefits as well. A heart-pounding workout or an almost meditative calm can be achieved with the use of the same simple piece of equipment.

Functional Fitness Training

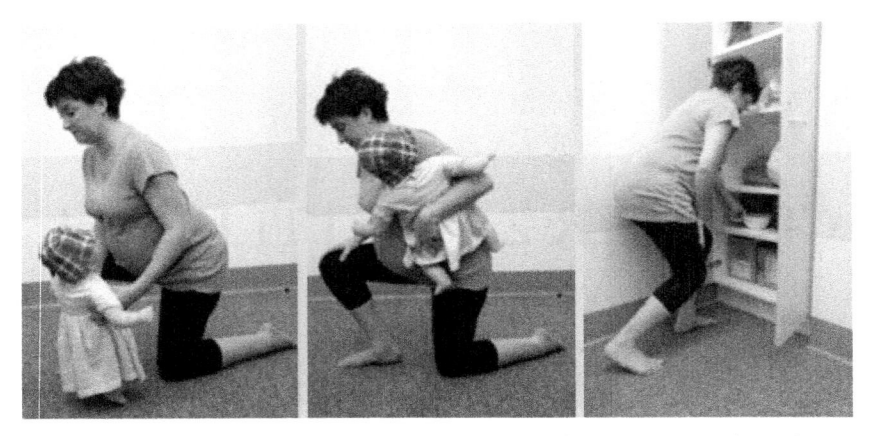

One of the greatest features involving the use of kettlebells is the **relationship to everyday activities**. This is called '*Functional Training*.' Most people don't exercise to improve sports performance – they do it to attain and maintain a certain level of fitness that is beneficial to their health. Functional fitness means that it is easier to perform the tasks involved in daily life and basic sports such as lifting, bending, squatting, stretching, and much more. By maintaining muscle strength, flexibility, and good balance, there is less likelihood of falling, straining a muscle, or suffering from any number of common injuries.

Another feature that makes working out with kettlebells so effective is the involvement of the entire body. Kettlebell workouts require much greater coordination between muscle groups than any other type of exercise so there is more toning, strengthening, and energy burning going on. From the simplest beginner moves to the fastest paced, advanced workouts, kettlebell exercises are adaptable for all purposes. This means that **kettlebells are the most efficient, effective workout equipment you can get.**

Kettlebell Training for Men

Great results in a shorter period of time make kettlebell training more and more attractive to busy men. Working with kettlebells provides a broader range of strength and fitness benefits and can easily be incorporated into any workout. Kettlebells, unlike barbells and exercise machines, are also easier to transport or store and can be used virtually anywhere.

Versatility is a key benefit to kettlebell training. It is perfect for casual fitness, as part of an athletic routine and even for competition. In other words, it can be adapted for all levels of fitness and designed for specific results. As a great all-around workout, kettlebell training does not interfere with sport-specific requirements but adds to the overall health and fitness of every individual. Different types of kettlebell training will be discussed in the next chapter.

Kettlebell Training for Women

Many women spend time and money searching for weight-loss and fitness programs only to be disappointed with the results. Kettlebell training is becoming increasingly popular with women because the results are quicker, easier to achieve and don't require expensive gym memberships.

Since time is a factor that limits everyone, women are particularly pleased with great toning and fat loss in shorter workouts. This is what has attracted many celebrities to kettlebell training programs! Because of the dynamic nature of working with kettlebells, **it is possible to burn up to 20 calories *per minute*, which means 400 calories in just a 20-minute workout**!

While men are most likely to pick up as much weight as they can, women tend to underestimate their capability. Since kettlebell movements are functional, mimicking daily activities, women quickly discover that they can handle much more weight than you would have expected. Just think about the typical things you do:

- Lift babies and small children
- Carry groceries and laundry baskets
- Stretch to vacuum, dust, and wash windows
- Bend and squat to do all sorts of cleaning and other chores

Also, think about how heavy your handbag or computer case may be, and you will realize that you are much stronger than you ever would have imagined.

Good form is a key to successful kettlebell training, and it is this attention to your position and movements that improves posture and tightens the core. The hip and pelvic movements needed to create the momentum of kettlebell swings are the best ways to firm and tone the butt for a great shape. What you learn and practice with the kettlebell transfers over to all your other motions and activities so that you are not only better able to avoid injury, but you will also look leaner.

One concern that many women have when the issue of resistance or weight training comes up is building bulk. With kettlebells, the cardiovascular benefits address weight loss, and the use of the weighted kettlebell helps boost fat loss without building muscle. Muscle tone is improved in general, but the main targets are the waist, hips, butt, and thighs and an overall increase in metabolic efficiency.

Osteoporosis is a major concern as women grow older, but strength training has been proven to combat issues that accompany lower bone density. Kettlebell training is a fun way to engage in this type of fitness and is much easier for most women than other types of weight-related exercise.

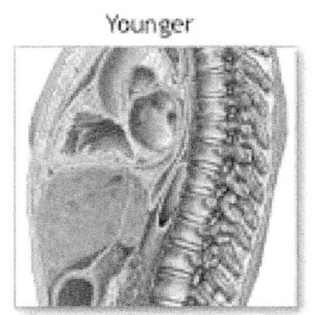

Normal spinal curvature

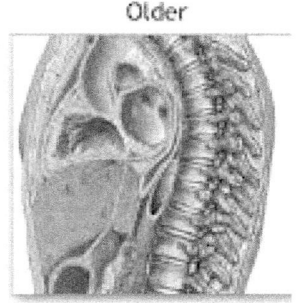

Spinal curvature degraded by bone and disk changes

Adapting Kettlebell Training for Specific Needs

Kettlebells are excellent tools for workouts of all kinds, even for rehabilitative exercises and physical therapy. This underscores the benefits of kettlebell training for a wide range of purposes with all types of people.

For athletes, kettlebell exercises can be developed to enhance flexibility and strength or to provide a balance to other parts of the body that are not specifically involved in that skill set. In an inclusive workout, general strength, balance, agility, and range of motion are all improved.

Training programs can also be designed for people with disabilities or those who are recovering after an injury or surgery. The movements are easier to learn and can be performed with less weight than activities involving barbells and are easily incorporated into circuit or interval training. The involvement of multiple muscle groups divides the stress of exercising and leads to a reduction of pain in the back, shoulders, and neck as long as the exercises are done properly.

CHAPTER 3 – KETTLEBELL TRAINING FOR EVERY PURPOSE

Kettlebell workouts are perfect for any number of purposes depending on your needs and ambitions. **Kettlebells can be incorporated into** virtually **every workout plan** for general fitness or designed for specific results, even physical therapy.

Cross training and *interval training* are popular methods for achieving great results, and it is quite simple to perform kettlebell workouts that fit these two styles. It is always best to check with your healthcare professional before beginning any new type of workout and learn the basics from a certified trainer to avoid possible injuries.

Cardio Workouts

The intensity of kettlebell workouts makes them perfect for the cardio aspect of any exercise program. One of the main reasons for this is the significant elevation of heart rate during kettlebell workouts even though calorie burn is equal to that of other types of cardio activities.

Another major plus for turning to kettlebells for cardio workouts is the relatively high *Rate of Perceived Exertion* (RPE). In controlled tests, **kettlebell activities** were **compared to treadmill work** and provided virtually identical results except for elevated heart rate. Although kettlebell workouts are felt to be more difficult, their uniqueness and all-around benefits actually made them more interesting and satisfying. Unless you are a dedicated athlete training for excellence, enjoying an activity is a critical factor in determining how long and how often it will be performed.

An added benefit of performing kettlebell swings and lifts for cardio workouts is the increase in lean muscle mass and core strengthening that lead to better overall fitness, stamina, and body tone. This type of routine also takes less time to achieve the same results as longer sessions on the treadmill or track.

Core Workouts

Kettlebell exercises are perfect for improving core strength and enhancing the strength and flexibility of all related muscles extending outward to the extremities. The reason for this is the fact that the shape and movement of the kettlebell at the end of your arm/s keeps you off balance and more muscles are required to stabilize your body. Since the kettlebell is not stationary in your hands, it adds to the dynamics of each movement, forcing your muscles to compensate for the changing center of gravity.

Unlike most other weight-training activities which isolate muscle groups, **kettlebell workouts require the cooperative coordination of all the core muscles as well as those in the shoulders and back**. You can control the intensity of the workout for losing weight or maintaining a good level of fitness all while conditioning and toning your core.

Cross Training

Working out by participating in a variety of activities has long been shown to have the most benefits for all-around fitness and health. Even among professional athletes where sport-dominant strength and flexibility are crucial, the results that come from a well-rounded training program have translated into better performance on the field.

Cross training at its simplest combines some type of cardio activity with one of the many strength-training workouts available. This contributes to better oxygenation during activity, overall muscular strength and endurance, and better general fitness. It also keeps the workout fresh and interesting since so many different options and combinations are possible.

Kettlebell training is the ideal combination of these two types of activities since it **involves the strength and coordination of many different muscles and can be as intense as you want for a heart-pounding cardio workout**. A tremendous variety of moves which can be done in numerous combinations are possible so kettlebell training can remain interesting in spite of using only one (or two) piece(s) of equipment.

Legs and Lower Body

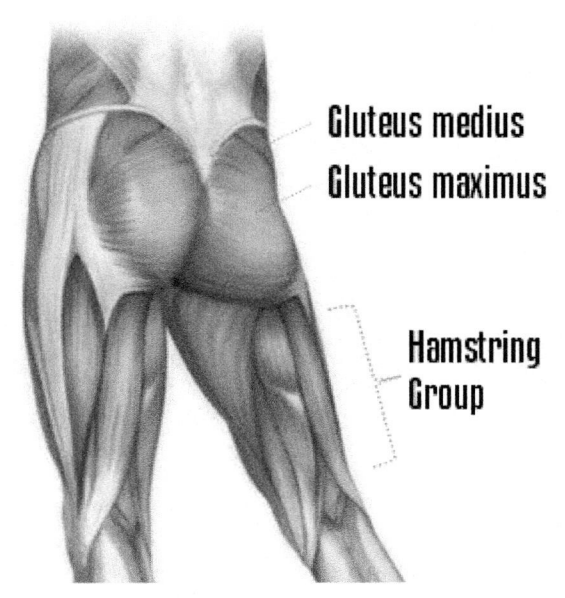

Weight lifters and athletes are quite familiar with barbell and dumbbell exercises for increasing lower body strength. For more of a variety and better overall results, kettlebell exercises strengthen and shape the legs, hips, and butt just as well, if not better! Power is especially important for a variety of sports, and the use of kettlebells improves an athlete's ability to move against resistance explosively.

Unlike traditional strength-training methods, using kettlebells coordinates the entire body, beginning with the core. **The legs, hips, and lower back become part of the overall movement** and can increase in strength and flexibility much more easily than with standard barbell and dumbbell lifts. The dynamic nature of the kettlebell swing provides more explosive strength without creating impact like plyometric exercises.

Strength

Kettlebells are available in a wide range of weights to accommodate the casual fitness enthusiast as well as the hard-core power lifter. Key factors that make kettlebells great for overall strength and conditioning is the variability in the grip and the planes of motion that are possible, unlike what you have with barbells or dumbbells.

Although it is not as easy to add weight to kettlebells, it is still possible to work through a program to increase size and strength with one kettlebell before moving on to a heavier kettlebell. Slowing the speed of the motions, cutting down the length of rest between sets, and holding your position between up and down movements provides a progressive increase in difficulty before reaching for a heavier weight.

The key for real strength is to lift more weight for a few reps instead of a lower weight for many reps. Of course, many athletes utilize both light and heavy workouts, but heavier training leads to greater endurance than just light workouts. Light, high-rep workouts are important, but they are not enough to produce the results you may want.

Toning and Shaping

Many people walk, jog, run, or perform some other type of cardio activity in order to lose or maintain weight. There is nothing wrong with that, but for real fitness, toning and shaping muscles is also important. Kettlebells provide a wonderful cardio workout but also contribute significantly to clearly defining muscles and trimming off excess fat.

The real benefit of muscle shaping comes after a kettlebell workout when the body works on repairing the muscle fibers and uses up tremendous amounts of calories. Since kettlebell workouts involve so many different muscles in a wide variety of stretches and positions, you are able to affect virtually all parts of the body during one workout by doing several different types of movements.

Swinging a kettlebell rhythmically is almost like dancing and can burn up to 20 calories a minute. This is an easy way to enjoy resistance training and saves a lot of time and effort compared to treadmill or other cardio activities, especially when you consider sports with similar caloric burn like uphill cross country skiing or running a six-minute mile.

Weight Loss

Weight loss is the main reason many people look for workout routines. Kettlebells are an excellent choice because they are effective for novices as well as advanced fitness enthusiasts with a variety of moves, weights, and programs to fit every purpose.

The primary factors that make any activity appropriate for weight loss include:

- **Increasing the metabolic rate**: The combined use of so many muscles requires vast energy supplies and that comes from revving up the metabolism.
- **Burning fat**: An improved metabolic rate means that the body needs an available source of energy and that comes from the excess fat stored in the cells and muscles.
- **"Afterburn"**: This is the desired effect of intense exercise! After a kettlebell workout, the body still demands energy and oxygen to return to equilibrium – homeostasis – by re-oxygenating tissues, refueling glycogen stores for normal cellular activity, and removing lactic acid and other cellular waste products.

Kettlebell workouts quickly bring your body to the fat-burning zone since you can involve hundreds of muscles while pumping up your heart rate. With the ability to burn up to 400 calories in a 20-minute workout and the added bonus of "afterburn," the weight will begin to drop off fairly quickly. Improved muscle tone allows the body to continually burn more calories and provides a better-looking body as well.

Physical Therapy and Rehabilitation

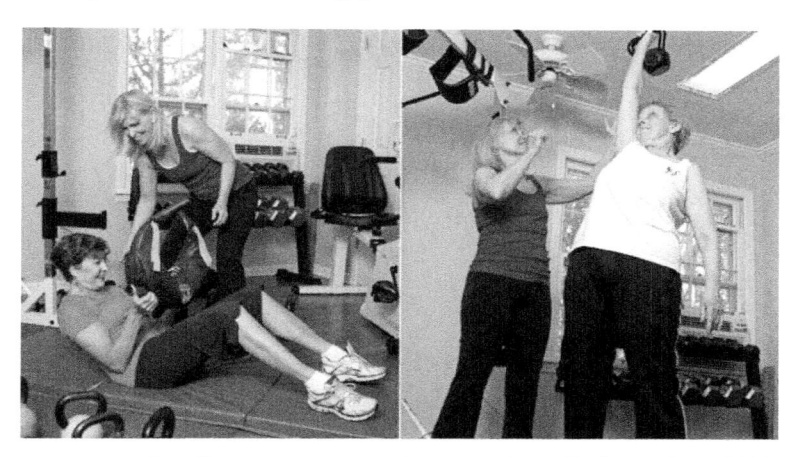

Anyone recovering from surgery or injury can benefit from the addition of kettlebell activities when they are able to add weight to stretching and range of motion exercises. The functional nature of kettlebell workouts offers a way to get back into shape performing movements that are at the core of daily activities and can be tailored to sport-specific requirements. The involvement of the core in virtually all kettlebell movements allows for the gentle working of injured areas unlike the specific muscular involvement associated with barbell, dumbbell, or machine workouts.

When a client is ready to add resistance to traditional squats or lunges, kettlebells can easily be used to add weight. Swinging motions that require acceleration and deceleration can be added for building strength. One of the greatest benefits of kettlebell exercises is the neurological conditioning provided during the functional movements. The nerves and neurological connections with muscles are re-programmed through repetition that mimics standard routines.

Once a patient is taught correct technique, the benefits of kettlebell training are almost immediate. Results are seen quickly with all-over toning and strengthening, and the programs are more interesting and enjoyable than traditional rehab routines. The cardio boost helps to release endorphins so that the session leaves you feeling mentally uplifted as well as less stiff and uncomfortable.

When deciding on following a regimen of kettlebell training for physical therapy or rehab, make sure that the clinician is a certified instructor. Only then can you be sure that you will be properly trained and monitored for the best results.

CHAPTER 4 – HOW TO CHOOSE THE RIGHT KETTLEBELL

Smooth Handle
No seams or burrs, so you will always have a strong and comfortable grip

Rust Resistant e-Coat
Inpenetrable coating prevents rust and corrosion caused by sweat and water

Solid Cast Iron
Ensures durability and lasting strength for years to come

Matte Black Finish

Weight Indicator

Kettlebells are very simple pieces of equipment with essentially very little variety in style. The only obvious differences between one make and the next are the **weight, shape of the handle,** and the **coating over the metal**. Initially, most kettlebells came from Russia, but there are many more manufacturers today that utilize a wide range of materials and have attempted design improvements.

Weight

The nature of kettlebell workouts is quite different than that of barbells or dumbbells, and the amount of weight used is also quite different. The free-moving flow of kettlebell lifts and swings and the resulting changes in the center of gravity depend on the cooperative effort of many different muscles unlike those used simply for strength. Experience has shown that women tend to underestimate the kettlebell weight they can work with while men initially over-estimate.

For casual fitness routines, most **women should start out with an 8 kg or *half a pood* (18 lb.) weight** (or just 4 kg (8 lb.) if you are older or have been inactive for a while) and **men with a 16 kg, *one pood* (35 lb.) kettlebell**. This depends on your overall fitness, comfort level, and goals. As you become proficient, or if you already are comfortable with such weight, you can progress to *12 kg (26 lb.), 16 kg (35 lb.), 20 kg (44 lb.),* and *24 kg (53 lb.)*. The best way to determine the weight you should purchase is to attend classes or find an instructor so you can see what works best for you.

Adjustable weight kettlebells are also available, but many experts suggest avoiding them in the interest of safety. Weight can be changed by adding or removing plates or filling/emptying sand or pebbles from inside the bell. Given the dynamic nature of kettlebell movements and the frequency of overhead positions, the chance of something falling on you is to be avoided. They can also be dangerous if the weight shifts within the bell and your grip and positioning has to change with every move.

Changing weights is not as important with kettlebell training as it is with barbells. With the same weight, you can increase the intensity of your workout with more reps, slower, increasing reps within a certain time period, and the addition of more difficult routines. In effect, you can actually use the same kettlebell for years!

If you are interested in **strength training**, body building, or competition, then progressing through increasing weight loads is important. Another option is to buy a second kettlebell of the same original weight for doubles training after you have become comfortable with the next one or two heavier bells.

Kettlebell Weight Selection Guidelines

FITNESS LEVEL		MEN	WOMEN
Novice	*Older adults, rehab from injury, petite body size*	8-12 kg	4-8 kg
Beginner	*New to a resistance workout, small build*	12-16 kg	8-12 kg
Intermediate	*Healthy, good fitness with some weight-training experience*	16-20 kg	12-16 kg
Advanced	*Healthy, athletic, experience with weight training, large build*	20-24 kg	16-20 kg

Shape and Size

Kettlebells are frequently referred to as cannon balls with handles. While that is a fairly accurate description, there is a bit more to the construction of a quality kettlebell. **The best bells are solid, one-piece construction made from a mold that includes the handle**. A kettlebell with a handle that is welded on can have seams or ridges that cause irritation to your hands and may even break apart!

Two **sides of a kettlebell** are flat so that the bell can rest more comfortably against the forearm in the racked position. The bottom is also flat so the bell stays in place when set down. Lesser quality kettlebells are often not completely flat at the base and wobble during exercises that use the bell as a ground fixture such as pushups.

Handles can be rounded or squared but should be large enough to accommodate your hand/s comfortably. There are some benefits to squared handles that form angles, but most instructors recommend curved or only somewhat flattened handles that can be gripped anywhere. Competition kettlebells have a slightly squared-off type of handle. The most important aspect of any handle, though, is its smooth connection to the bell.

Depending on the make of the kettlebell, **sizes** may be uniform as the weights increase or increase with added weight. Handle dimensions may also change. The benefit of same-size kettlebells such as those used in competition is that your positioning will always be the same (except for natural bracing to accommodate a heavier weight). In other words, the bell will sit on your arm in the same way no matter what the weight. If you work with bells that are different sizes, you have to adjust your grip and positioning to take the added dimensions into consideration.

KETTLEBELL TRAINING

Materials and Finishes

PORTABLE KETTLE BELL SANDBAG™

- Molded grip - Lifetime Warranty
- 1.5" Webbing - 2,000+ lb tensile strength
- 1050d Ballistic Nylon
- Solid-panel construction
- Handmade in the U.S.A.
- Side-release buckle
- Wide-mouth for easy filling
- Bonded Nylon thread

- Patent pending design
- Puncture, tear, abrasion, UV resistant
- Dry-bag design - no zippers, no jams
- Use any filler: sand, stones, chains, buckshot...

Traditionally, kettlebells were made from *cast iron*. While that is still the case with some of the top kettlebells made today, professional-grade bells are made from *stainless steel*. Some newer makes use a hard, rubber-like material, and there are also *iron-sand-filled neoprene bags* of different weights. Lower grade kettlebells are available that are made from a variety of materials, but many of these are not as durable as metal bells. Some brands containing bearings and swivels site convenience in their marketing, but nothing beats the good old standard.

For the sake of appearance, some kettlebells are covered with colored vinyl. This helps differentiate bells of different weights but can cause friction on the hands during some moves if the vinyl also covers the handle. These covers are said to protect surfaces, and this may be true for scratches, but dropping a kettlebell can cause damage to virtually any flooring. Most cast iron kettlebells are natural black, but many brands are painted or powder coated.

Most experts consider an unpainted, sanded metal handle to be the best for grip. The surface should be smooth but not glassy so that chalk will stick and help your hold.

Some kettlebells come with a rubberized ring around the bottom, also for the protection of surfaces, but this can be uncomfortable when pressed against the arm.

Brands of Kettlebells

There are a number of kettlebell manufacturers so it is important to check on the brand's quality before making a purchase. A general rule of thumb is **to avoid purchasing kettlebells from box stores** because they tend to be less well made to sell for a lower price. You will have to pay for quality, but some brands are more reasonable than others.

- *Ader Pro-Grade* – These competition bells are color coded and have bare steel handles that are 33 mm in diameter. Being competition kettlebells means they are the exact same size regardless of the bell's weight.

- *Ader* – These non-competition bells are a popular option among common kettlebells. They can be purchased from a variety of retailers, even in sets, and are a solid, reliable bell.
- *American Kettlebell Club*
- *Apollo* – These also come with a rubber pad.
- *CAP*
- *RKC Dragon Door Russian Kettlebells* – Some people swear by these popular kettlebells. This quality brand is also available on Amazon, where Prime members can get a good deal with shipping.
- *Eleiko*
- *Fringe Sport* – Ranging from 4 kg to 48 kg (9-106 pounds) the FringeSport OFW Kettlebells are both affordable and have most of the features needed. They have a flat bottom, accurate weight measurements (in kg), and they come in one piece, with seamless casting and handles big enough for two hands even on the smaller units. They have a durable finish that holds chalk and is appropriate for long, CrossFit-style sets. The FringeSport kettlebells are also offered with free shipping.

KETTLEBELL TRAINING

- *Gold's*
- *Life Line*
- *Punch*
- *Rogue* – This brand offers their bells in weights ranging from 9 pounds to over 200. With their black powder-coated finish and color strip around the base, to denote the bell's weight, they are kettlebells with a unique look.

Most of these brands are available for purchase worldwide; however, some countries offer their own designed kettlebells of superb quality. One of the examples is *Wolverson kettlebells* which are produced and designed in the UK.

CHAPTER 5 – KETTLEBELL STYLE, FORM, AND TECHNIQUE

Working with kettlebells requires proper form and an understanding of posture, grip, balance, and transitions. Just as with any type of exercise equipment, learning how to use kettlebells correctly is important for success and to avoid injury. While there are excellent DVDs available, working with a certified instructor for at least a few lessons is the best way to ensure a complete understanding of style and technique and to correct any aspect of your use of the kettlebell that may be harmful.

Before beginning any workout program, it is also a good idea to check with your healthcare professional to rule out any issues that may prevent you from getting the most you can out of the experience.

Style

Three different styles of kettlebell lifting are popular today, and each provides slightly different results.

Hard Style: Considered the 'original' kettlebell workout, hard style involves generating explosive power and strength. Hard style is best defined by the 'Kime' technique, where an all-out effort is applied during each rep. Producing the power needed to swing, snatch, press, or squat is the goal and increasing that power is the key. Also called the '*Russian Kettlebell Challenge*,' hard style kettlebell lifting utilizes fast, rigid movements that appear 'jerky' based on the principle of repeated relaxation and tension as opposed to looking smooth and fluid. Hard style's goals are to maximize relaxation/speed and tension/strength. Because muscles create more force the more they tense, dynamic tension helps when performing the press and squat (slow strength lifts). **Hard style helps you get stronger with harder muscle contraction**. And, it forces you to practice relaxation. It has been determined that as athletes level, relaxing the muscles happens more quickly. So, don't hold back. Make sure every rep counts. Then, every following workout results in more output more quickly.

Sport Style: Also known as *Girevoy* (from the Russian word for kettlebell) *Sport* (GS) or *Fluid Style*, sport style combines power and strength for overall endurance. GS lifters work with a submaximal load competing in timed lifts in 3 main disciplines – the jerk, the long cycle clean and jerk, and the snatch. (These moves will be discussed in Chapter 6.) An efficient technique is the key to sport style lifting so that the movements can be maintained for 10 minutes. **Sport style instructs you to perform with a submaximal load, to perform as many kettlebell lift reps as you can in 10 minutes**.

Juggling: Although the idea of juggling an iron or steel ball weighing more than 10 or 20 pounds over your head may seem insane, it has become a very popular form of kettlebell lifting. In addition to the usual benefits of kettlebell workouts, juggling provides for increased ability in:

- Core strength and resistance to rotation
- Powerful pulling strength
- Hand-eye coordination
- Reaction speed
- Fun!

KETTLEBELL TRAINING

Another style of kettlebell training that can be mentioned is the *American Style* that is incorporated into CrossFit.

Holds

Although a kettlebell looks quite simple, it can actually be held and used in a number of different ways to achieve a tremendous range of results. Each grip, crush, grab, hold, and angle changes the muscles being used as well as the difficulty of basic moves. Using one hand or two with one bell or doubles also provides different results.

Racked: An integral part of many kettlebell exercises is the "Rack" position. In this position, the arm is bent with the upper arm held tight to the body and the hand in line with the chin. The handle is in your palm, and the bell is on the outside of your arm. A reverse rack is essentially the same but with the bell on the inside of the arm.

By the Horns: A common position for beginners is holding the kettlebell by the "horns" or sides of the handle. The bell should be held close to the chest, roughly at mid-chest with the bottom facing up or down.

Squeeze or Crush: This is similar to "by the horns," but instead of gripping the horns, support the bell by squeezing it with the base of your fingers (where they join the palm). This involves the use of other arm muscles to compensate for the lack of grip.

Waiter: The kettlebell simply rests in your open palm.

The image below shows the modified waiter hold with the thumb inside the handle.

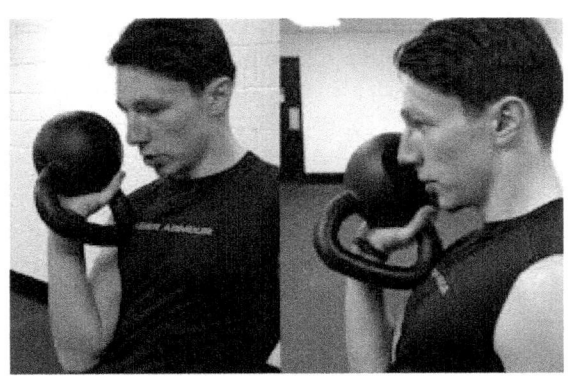

Foot in the Handle: With your toes through the handle, it is possible to work a variety of leg muscles.

There are a variety of other holds that use these same principles for a tremendous range of movements that target virtually every muscle. An important consideration with any of them is to **keep your wrists neutral** – not bent forward or back – and a secure but not deathly grip so that the bell swivels as it needs to.

Posture

Maintaining the appropriate posture is extremely important when exercising with kettlebells in order to prevent injury to the lower back, shoulders, and neck. It is not complicated but can never be compromised for the sake of more weight or a certain number of repetitions. This is called '*training to failure*' and refers to the inability to perform the motions properly due to exhaustion.

The primary consideration during kettlebell workouts is to **avoid hunching forward with rounded shoulders**. While keeping the shoulders packed (tightly in the socket), the head should be facing forward with the eyes focused roughly 6 feet ahead, down toward the ground. The spine should retain its natural 'S' curve as if you are about to sit down on a chair – the knees bent, the hips lowered, and the butt back. You should be able to place a stick along your spine from your head to your hips with contact between the stick and your head, shoulders, and upper glutes.

There is a **tendency** for people to try **to 'muscle' the kettlebell with upper body strength**. This puts the shoulders, neck, and lower back at risk by ignoring the power of the hips, legs, and gluteal muscles which provide the force for swings.

Footwear plays a key role in how the body balances, and for that reason, wearing thin shoes with flat soles (like wrestling shoes) or working barefoot is preferred. The muscles and nerves in your feet help signal other muscles to tighten or loosen as needed to support the body and the movements of the kettlebell.

During kettlebell swings and lifts, **the feet** must remain firmly planted on the floor. The heels should not rise up (in almost all cases) because the power is concentrated in the legs and hips. Working on dirt or sand – as long as it is firm and flat – allows the feet to take advantage of their natural ability to grip.

Safety Tips

Learning to use a kettlebell properly with the help of an instructor is the best way to safeguard your health and the integrity of your gym or home. As with any type of lifting activity, there is always a risk of back or shoulder injury so the correct form is necessary. A few **key points to keep in mind** will enable you **to get the most out of your kettlebell workouts**:

1. Make sure there is enough space around you to swing the kettlebell without interference.
2. Warm up like you would before any type of lifting activity to avoid injuries.
3. Practice all moves without a weight first to ensure proper form before working out with the kettlebell.
4. Choose a lighter weight as opposed to a heavier one if you have a question.
5. Use chalk, keep a towel handy to wipe away sweat, or wear gloves to protect your hands.
6. Start with the most basic moves and master them before attempting more complex exercises.
7. Always focus on maintaining a neutral spine and the right stance with heels firmly on the floor. Wearing the appropriate footwear is a critical factor for the best balance.
8. Never attempt to 'muscle' the kettlebell with the upper body, shoulders, or arms! Your strength must come from the hips and legs.
9. Avoid forcing reps or training to muscle failure because you lose the ability to maintain proper form. This can lead to injuries.
10. Concentrate on controlling the kettlebell to avoid gripping too tightly or alternately smashing the forearms.

Another aspect of kettlebell training safety is **knowing when to take a break**. Just like any other type of intense training, kettlebell workouts progress so far and then a *plateau* is reached. In many cases, taking some time off and then starting up again at a slightly lower intensity is the way to break past that barrier.

Short-term breaks are simply taking a day or more off between workouts to avoid over-exercising. Some people can handle 5 or 6 days of training each week, but others may be better off working out every other day. This allows the body the opportunity to adjust to the demands you are making on it and grow stronger.

A longer-term break is a great way to add variety to your training schedule while you let your body rest from the continued stress of lifting and swinging. It is a proactive way of letting your muscles grow and adjust since you could be forced into a break due to injury. Participating in another discipline such as yoga, swimming, or a martial art keeps you active but gives your body a chance to recover from intense heavy workouts.

Shoulder packing is a specific practice that needs to be mastered for overall success. This concept will be discussed in detail in the next chapter but is mentioned here since it is crucial for the health and safety of the shoulders and back. It is a practice that must be incorporated in all kettlebell activities as part of proper form.

The Importance of Active Recovery

Active recovery is simply performing some other activity while taking a rest during heavy workouts. This can be done on 'off days' or within an individual training session. The major benefit of this relatively recent trend is to allow the heart rate to remain elevated while removing lactic acid and metabolic wastes that accumulate in the muscles during heavy lifting or intense workouts.

There are several additional reasons **why engaging in active recovery during a workout is beneficial**:

- Blood continues to be pushed back to the heart so the heart does not have to work as hard.
- Muscles stay warm so resuming intense activity isn't a shock.
- Maintaining some type of activity keeps your mind in the game – you don't start thinking about what you have to do later.

As far as **active recovery during a kettlebell workout** is concerned, it can be some stretches, a mobility activity, or another light exercise with a lighter weight or no weight.

CHAPTER 6 – THE FUNDAMENTALS OF KETTLEBELL EXERCISES

Kettlebells have been around for a long time but only recently have they become a staple at the gym or fitness center. Although technically simple, **it is imperative to perform kettlebell moves carefully and in proper form**. That is the best way to get the most out of your workout and avoid any type of injury, especially to the back or shoulders.

Before You Begin

As with any new exercise or diet program, it is important to check with your healthcare professional. The next step is to learn about the activities you will be engaging in so that you can perfect the form. For the greatest success with kettlebell training, there are key factors to consider as the basis for all further training: abdominal bracing and perfecting the hip hinge.

Abdominal bracing is exactly what the name implies – bracing the muscles in the core, lower back, and buttocks all at the same time to ensure spinal stability and protect the discs. Mastering this concept will increase the effectiveness of all your subsequent workouts as well as increase the protection of your spine.

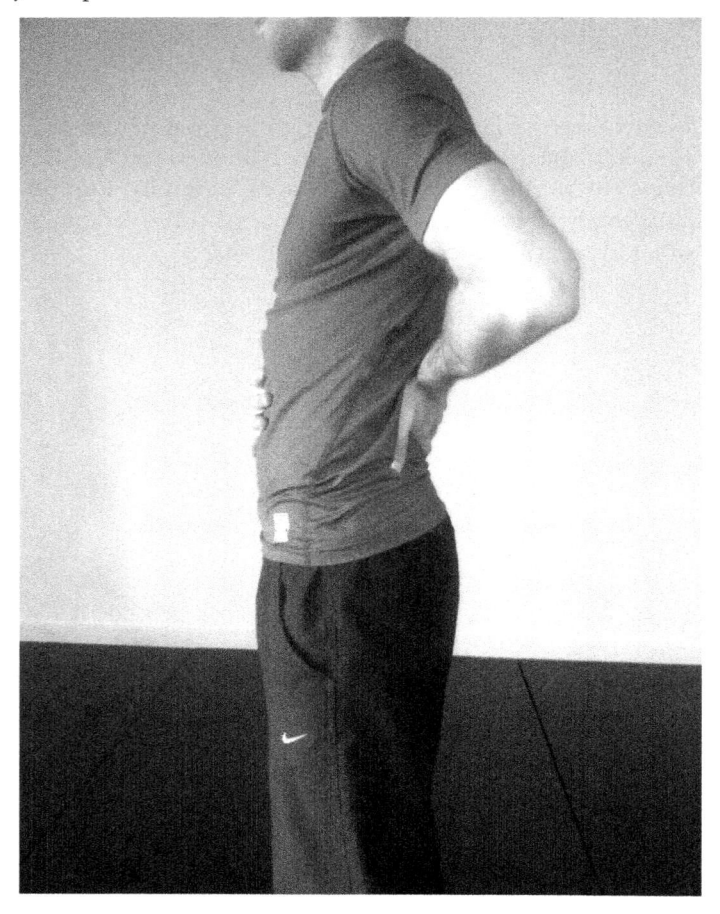

- Stand up straight with your feet shoulder width apart.

- Place one hand on your abdomen and the other on the small of your back.
- Contract your abdominal muscles (suck them in) as if you are about to be punched.
- Increase the contraction and then contract the muscles in the buttocks (as if you are holding in a bowel movement).
- Hold the contractions for 10 seconds, then release.

While you are practicing abdominal bracing, it is important to maintain a relaxed diaphragm so that you can breathe normally. You should be able to walk and talk normally while performing this activity. For more advanced practice, this can be done lying on your back or while holding a bridge position supporting yourself on your forearms and toes.

The hip hinge movement is the key to proper kettlebell lifting and swinging as well as the source of strength and power for effective kettlebell workouts. Understanding the proper mechanics behind the hip hinge is important so that the movement becomes completely natural.

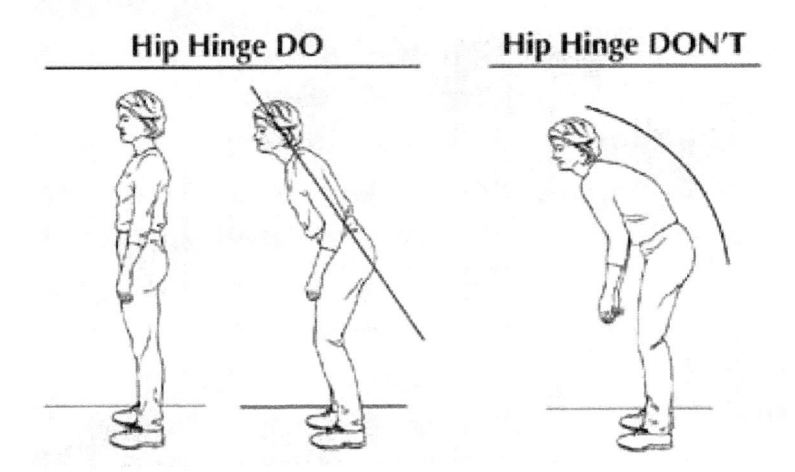

Hip Hinge DO | Hip Hinge DON'T

There are several 'tests' to ***ensure that you are performing the hip hinge correctly***:

1. **Kneeling Hip Isolation**: For the easiest introduction to the hip hinge, kneel on the floor with your arms out in front and bring your butt back to your heels and raise up again. You don't need to move anything else since the hips perform the entire action. Maintain a straight back with your head in line.

2. **Tap the Wall**: With your feet shoulder width apart, stand with your back about 1 foot away from a wall. Place the edge of each hand (the pinky side) along the creases in the groin and push your hips back by tightening your abs and glutes until you touch the wall with your butt without significantly bending your knees. Your weight should be on your heels so that the wall is not providing you with any support. Bring your hips forward and return to a standing position. (Something easier to picture, perhaps, is to take the stance of a baseball shortstop – pelvis back with hands just above the knees.)

   As this becomes 'easy' to do, inch slightly farther away from the wall always making sure to maintain a neutral spine.

3. **Deadlift**: Again, with your feet shoulder width apart and a kettlebell on the floor between them, reach back with your hips until your hands are lowered to the kettlebell. Grasp the kettlebell handle and lean slightly towards it without rounding the shoulders or bending at the waist. Reverse your movement to stand up, pressing against your heels as you tighten the glutes and 'unhinge' the hips. For the deadlift as well as virtually all kettlebell movements, keep your arms tight to your rib cage and maintain a firm but loose grip. (To prevent having to bend the knees as you reach for the kettlebell, place the kettlebell on a stable elevated surface such as an upturned dumbbell or small stool.)

   This motion is the basis for all grind exercises which will be explained in the next section.

KETTLEBELL TRAINING

A   B

4. **Simple Swing**: Place the kettlebell on the floor about your foot's length in front of you and get down to it the same way you did in the Deadlift. Taking the slack out of your body (tensing yourself as you lean slightly toward the kettlebell), hike the bell back between your legs as forcefully as you can. Remember to maintain a neutral back and balance with your weight on your heels. Bring the kettlebell forward to the starting position and set it down.

The swing is the basic motion used in all ballistic kettlebell movements.

5. **Continuous Swing**: Instead of returning to the starting position as in the Simple Swing, you will now complete a set of continuous, fluid swings. The downward motion is the same as in the previous activities, but now, you will continue with the kettlebell swinging up in front of you as you tighten the glutes, maintain braced abs, and keep your legs engaged with your shoulders back and down and a neutral spine.

These exercises are a progression designed to be mastered in order. The better you maintain the correct posture and a stable core, the easier each of the following steps will be.

One way to test for the 'neutral spine' position is to hold a dowel or length of PVC pipe along your back. If you have 3-point contact at all times, you are doing it correctly. The back of the head, the upper back, and the top of the glutes must be touching the line throughout the movement. This helps to show you if you are incorrectly rounding or arching your back, lowering or flexing your head, or hunching your shoulders.

General hip mobility ensures the widest range of motion so that all relevant muscles can be properly activated. Hip flexor muscles and hamstrings are frequently tight and can seriously impede your ability to move well during kettlebell workouts as well as cause other muscles to compensate. It is this type of adjustment that ruins form and can lead to injury, especially in the lower back.

Hip flexors can easily tighten up after extended periods of sitting or by not stretching properly after exercising.

Several ways to loosen hip flexors include:

- Standing with feet shoulder width apart, alternately bring your knees to your chest as if you are marching in place slowly. Perform 5 to 10 lifts with each leg, trying to reach a bit higher with each knee lift.

- Sitting up in a straight chair holding the sides for balance, straighten one leg out in front of you and keep the other foot flat on the floor. Raise the straight leg up to waist level. Lower the leg to parallel and then the starting position and repeat 10 to 15 times before switching to the other leg.

- In a deep lunge position, tilt your pelvis forward while bracing your abs. This will stretch the back of the upper thigh. Instead of tilting the pelvis forward, you can also rotate the hips in a circular motion supporting yourself with both hands on the floor inside of your forward knee.

The hamstrings are commonly the cause of sports injuries so keeping them loose is quite important. Just like tight hip flexors, tight hamstrings prevent the full range of motion of the pelvis, and other muscles are called into action to compensate. Unfortunately, there are several different conditions that cause hamstring tightness and each requires a different type of exercise for release. In each situation, however, the underlying problem is the inappropriate tilt of the pelvis due to either poor posture (an anterior pelvic tilt common among women), or a posterior tilt as a result of extended periods of sitting with bent knees. Another cause is lumbar disc issues, so this is a perfect example of the importance of checking with a medical professional.

- Lie flat on your back and wrap a towel around one foot. Using the towel for support, pull your leg up straight close to perpendicular and even farther if possible. Alternate legs. Similarly, you can lie on the floor in a doorway with one leg up straight against the wall. Move your hips further into the doorway to increase the stretch.

- In a sitting position with your legs extended straight out in front, bend at the waist keeping your back straight and reach for your toes. Don't bounce but hold the stretch for at least 30 to 60 seconds. Return slowly to a sitting position using a tight core and repeat.
- With just one leg out straight in front of you on the floor, bring the other foot in to rest against the thigh of the straight leg. Reach with both hands for the toes of the extended leg.
- Stand with your right foot crossed in front of the left and gently bend from the waist without bending your knees to touch your toes, trying to bring your forehead to your knee.

Shoulder packing refers to the tight connection of the upper arm bone to the shoulder socket, and this is accomplished with the help of many different muscles. In this position, you have the greatest strength, but as the gap widens, the muscles become weaker and the risk of injury increases. To understand the concept of packing and compensate during overhead presses, begin with a light weight and imagine that it is heavier. Stretching the opposite arm out to the side with a fist and pulling inward, as if you are resisting someone pulling on you, will help keep the lifting shoulder packed through a move. It is important to keep the shoulders down, away from the ears during all lifts and not try to 'hunch' them up. When fatigue causes you to lose the ability to pack the shoulders, you must stop the exercise to prevent injury.

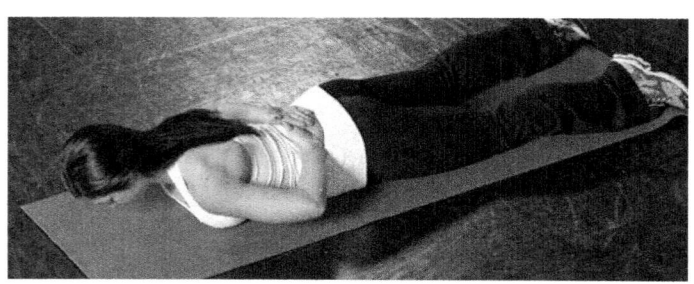

Breathing is an important aspect for performing any type of exercise. With kettlebell workouts, the general rule is that ***breathing comes before movement*** and is best done as an ***inhale through the nose and exhale through the mouth***. This explosive exhale aids in bracing the core and helps in the active part of the exercise. For example, during a kettlebell squat, inhale as you squat and then exhale explosively to stand up. During swings, inhale as you thrust the hips forward and the kettlebell up and exhale as you lower the bell. This takes advantage of the natural openness and then constriction of the lungs and diaphragm. Maintaining deep, even breaths is important to maintain strength, reduce stress, and remove metabolic wastes that build up in the muscles during exercise.

Understanding the Terms

The Rack Position is a position where the arm/s are bent, elbows pointing straight down and fists aimed towards your chin. This position forms a universal base for all kettlebell exercises. As you hold the bell/s on the flat of your palm, your upper arm keeps contact with your torso. The kettlebell should be touching both the upper and lower arm as well as the chest. This should be performed with a rather narrow stance with your knees locked and thighs relaxed.

The Swing is a position where your shoulder/s act as a hinge, creating a back-and-forth movement with the arm/s while the kettlebell moves like a pendulum. Your abs should be braced, your back slightly arched, and the hips hinged. This can be done with one or two hands on one kettlebell or with two hands and two kettlebells.

KETTLEBELL TRAINING

The Clean is a swinging action with the kettlebell, then catch the bell in the Rack position. It is the beginning of a variety of other exercises involving overhead lifts.

The Jerk is performed from the chest and/or Clean position. Your upper arm is kept tight against the body, and your legs are kept straight. While pressing the kettlebell/s overhead with power from your legs, the torso, arms, and legs need to be kept straight.

The Snatch takes advantage of a full swing to an over-the-head position. The power of the lift comes from the hips and the tightening of the glutes, locking the body for stability. As the kettlebell rises above chest height, dip at the knees and remember to grip the handle tightly to control the impact against the forearm.

CHAPTER 7 – 30 BASIC KETTLEBELL EXERCISES AND HOW TO PERFORM THEM

When you are ready to begin kettlebell exercises, choose the weight that provides resistance without causing you to strain. It is more **important to perform the moves correctly with a lower weight** than to risk injury by trying to use too much weight.

For athletic women, an 8 to 12 kg weight is a good place to start, and for men, a 16 kg weight is good.

Trying several weights can be a good idea before buying a particular size.

There are 2 key moves to master that are the basis for all other kettlebell workouts. For Grinds, the slow, full-body power moves, the deadlift is fundamental. ***Adjust your rate of lift to be able to complete at least 10 reps without exhaustion.*** Moving too quickly sacrifices form, and moving too slowly compromises balance.

Grind workouts include:

- Squats
- Windmills
- Overhead Presses
- Rows
- Turkish Get Up

Ballistic exercises are the dynamic, multi-joint motions that incorporate many different muscles and muscle groups simultaneously and are all based on the swing. The speed of ballistic movements will be determined by the thrust of your hips and the weight of the bell. Avoid forcing the motion by trying to use your arms because that interrupts the true flow of the movement.

Ballistic workouts include:

- Swings
- Pulls
- Cleans
- Snatch
- Russian Twists

Almost all of these exercises can be done in a number of different ways – with one hand, two hands, or one or two kettlebells in one or each hand. With that in mind, though, it must be stated again that the **basic forms of kettlebell lifting and swinging must be mastered** before moving on to anything more complex.

Another important factor to keep in mind is to **vary the types of exercises you include in your workout**. Because of the intense nature of most of these moves, you need to be sure to address corresponding muscles and muscle groups to avoid over-developing one set and causing pain or injury in another set due to a limited range of motion.

Grind Exercises

Deadlift

- With a heavy kettlebell (the next weight up from your usual working weight) on the floor in front of you, stand with your feet at hip width.
- Drop your hips by bending your knees to pick up the weight while keeping your back straight and shoulders down.
- Keep your abs braced and head in line (eyes focused ahead about 6 feet) and pick up the weight.
- Return to the standing position using the power of the hips and legs.
- Repeat for 8 to 10 reps.

One-Legged Deadlift

A   B

- Stand with a heavy kettlebell in both hands or one in each.
- Maintaining good form – back straight, shoulders back, and abs braced – tip forward from the hips lowering the weight to the floor as you lift one leg up and back until your torso and leg are parallel to the floor.
- Lower the leg and stand, returning to starting position, and complete 8 to 10 reps before switching legs.

Squats

- With two hands on one kettlebell (or one in each hand for more advanced practice), stand with feet hip width apart.
- Brace the abs, hold the torso upright and the back straight, and bend the knees with control so the weight dangles to the floor. (Remember that the movement is coming from the lowering of your hips and butt, and your calves are straight up and down.)
- Squeeze the glutes together to initiate upward movement, keeping the abs tight.

Goblet Squat

- Take the bell by the horns, holding at chest level, and stand with your feet at shoulder width.
- Lower your butt and hips, squatting downward as if sitting on a chair. Remember to keep your head and chest up and your back straight throughout the exercise.
- At the lowest point, press through your feet and use your hips to return to a standing position.

Kettlebell Front Squat

- Hold a kettlebell in the racked position, in front of the shoulder.
- Stretch out the opposite arm for balance and engage your core.
- Squat by thrusting your butt and hips back until your thighs are parallel to the floor. (That's the height to aim for!)
- Press against your heels and stand up, repeating for a total of 8 to 10 reps, then switch sides.

Kettlebell Squat Thrusts (Burpees)

- Squat and grasp a heavy kettlebell in a 'squeeze' hold (hands firmly grasping the sides of the bell). Make sure you are balanced.
- Step the legs back into a plank position maintaining straight, strong wrists. (A more advanced move is to jump both legs back together.)
- Bring the feet back to the start position (in a squat) and stand up. (For added exercise, lift the kettlebell from the handle as you stand.)
- Repeat for a total of 8 to 10 reps.

Kettlebell Windmill

- Hold a kettlebell in one hand with the toes on that side pointing out and the opposite foot pointing forward.
- Raise the opposite arm straight up from the shoulder as you lean with the kettlebell, slightly bending the knee on the kettlebell side. Push the opposite hip out.
- Keep both arms straight, looking up at the raised hand for an extra challenge, and return to start, and alternate sides for a total of 8 to 10 reps on each side.

Kettlebell Lunge

- Stand up straight, feet hip width apart with your abs braced and shoulders relaxed. Take the bell in your hand and have your palm face your body. (Or, hold it with both hands in front or one in each hand.)
- Step back with the leg on the opposite side of the kettlebell and lower the front knee.
- As you lower into the lunge, pass the bell through the middle of your legs and switch hands.
- Return to the standing position by stepping forward from the back leg and repeat the move with the switched hand to complete one full rep. Complete a total of 10 to 20 reps.

Kettlebell Reverse Lunge

- Stand up straight, feet hip width apart with your abs braced and shoulders relaxed. Take the bell in your hand, or both hands, and have your palm face your body.
- Step forward with the opposite foot and bend the knee.
- Return to a standing position by pushing against the front foot and stepping it back to meet the other foot. Switch feet to complete one rep.

One Arm Press

- Hold a kettlebell in one hand, extending the other hand out for balance as you lower into a squat.
- Brace the abs, keep the torso upright, and make sure the calves are perpendicular.
- In this position, push the bell up slowly, rotating the palm out so the bell is across the palm against the top of your forearm.
- Remember to keep the abs braced and avoid arching the back!
- Slowly bring the arm down, rotating the palm so your palm is facing in.
- Complete 8 to 10 reps with each side.

One Arm Military Press

- Stand with feet shoulder width apart and bring the kettlebell into rack position.
- Raise the bell overhead keeping your arm in as close to your head as possible. (It is important to have good posture and don't bounce as you lift.)
- Lower the kettlebell, again keeping the fist as close to your face as possible, ideally just in front of your cheek.
- Continue lowering the bell to place it on the floor to count as one complete rep. Repeat for 8 to 10 reps and then switch sides.

Two Arm Military Press

- Clean press two kettlebells to your shoulders, palms facing in toward the face. Remember to stabilize your core, contract your butt and lats.
- Press the kettlebells up to an overhead position, leaning into the weight. Keep arms as close to upright as possible.
- Return to the inward shoulder position and repeat.

Halo

- Stand with feet shoulder width apart. Hold a lighter kettlebell with two hands in front of one hip.
- Lift the kettlebell diagonally to the opposite shoulder, continuing the motion over your head.
- Circle the kettlebell around the back of your head and bring it down to the opposite hip from your starting point.
- Keep your core braced and back straight.

Kettlebell Rows

- Hold a kettlebell in one hand, stretching the other to the side for balance.
- Bend at the waist and bend the knees to protect the lower back.
- Using the back muscles, pull the elbow up to torso level, then slowly straighten out the arm.
- Complete 8 to 10 reps and then switch sides.

Kettlebell Pushup

- In a pushup position (on knees or toes), with hands shoulder width apart, place one hand on a kettlebell – on the bell itself or on the handle for a greater level of difficulty.
- Lower yourself making sure to brace the abs, keep the torso stiff, and the back straight.
- Be careful not to strain the shoulder of the arm on the kettlebell and push back up.
- Complete 8 to 10 reps and switch sides.

Renegade Rows

A

B

- Assume a standard pushup position with feet spread slightly wider than usual and a kettlebell on the floor between your hands. (The picture shows this being done with two hands gripping the handles of two kettlebells, but this is a highly advanced move!)
- While forcing pressure down on one hand, grip the handle of the kettlebell with the other hand and bring it up to your chest.
- Return to the pushup position and lift the opposite side for a total of 8 to 10 reps each.

Modified Turkish Get Up

Turkish Half Get-Up
Step 1

Turkish Half Get-Up
Step 2

Turkish Half Get-Up
Step 3

- Lie on your back holding a kettlebell in one hand with the arm extended straight up and the elbow locked. Keep your eyes on the kettlebell throughout the exercise.
- Looking at the bell and keeping the arm extended upwards, rise up onto your opposite elbow. At the same time, bend the knee (on the kettlebell side).
- Continue pushing up to your hand.
- Hold the 'pose' and then return to the prone position by straightening the lower leg, unbending the knee, and lowering the shoulders to the floor all while keeping the kettlebell extended.

Turkish Get Up

- Lie on your back holding a kettlebell in one hand with the arm extended straight up and the elbow locked. Keep your eyes on the kettlebell throughout the exercise.
- Looking at the bell and keeping the arm extended upwards, rise up onto your opposite elbow. At the same time, bend the knee (on the kettlebell side).
- Continue pushing up to your hand while moving the foot of your straight leg under the bent leg.
- Follow through to a standing position with the arm continually extended up over your head.
- Reverse the procedure to return to a prone position on the floor and complete 8 to 10 reps before switching arms.

This exercise is best mastered without holding any weight so you can develop fluid movements.

Supine Bridge

- Lie on your back with your knees bent and your arms along your sides. Place a kettlebell on your belly button (after you have practiced the move to perfect your form and build up some stamina).
- With a tight core, lift your torso so that your weight is distributed between your feet, shoulders, and upper back.
- Return to the starting position and complete 10 to 12 reps for one set.

Farmer's Walk

- Place kettlebells to the sides of your feet, squat down, and lift them keeping your back straight, shoulders back, face forward, and abs braced.
- Walk forward for a predetermined distance, beginning with 25 yards and working up to 200 yards. Use smaller steps to complete the distance if you begin to get tired.
- Return the kettlebells to the ground, rest, and repeat, starting with 2 sets several times a week, then adding an extra set every week or two until you can cover the distance performing 10 sets. After 10 sets, increase the distance dropping back to 2 sets and working up again.

Ballistic Exercises

One Arm Swing

- Instead of holding a kettlebell with two hands, hold it with one while extending the other arm to the side for balance.
- Use your hips and legs for thrust, bringing the weight to waist level and work up to extending the swing to shoulder height.
- Work one side for 8 to 10 reps, then switch to the other side.

Two Arm Swing

- Grip a kettlebell with both hands, standing with feet spread to hip width.
- Squat with your arms touching your inner thighs. Remember to push back with your butt and maintain a neutral back.
- At the bottom of the squat, add pressure to your heels and push your hips forward to stand.
- Bring the kettlebell up to hip level to begin with until you can comfortably continue the movement up to shoulder level.
- When the kettlebell reaches the top of the swing, it should feel weightless since the power and momentum is coming from your hips and legs.
- As the kettlebell returns to a hanging position, squat and repeat the steps for 8 to 10 reps.

Alternating Swing

- Using the form for a one arm swing with the opposite arm held along your side instead of extended, switch hands at the top of each swing at the point where the kettlebell feels weightless.
- Begin with 8 to 10 reps, then do another set or two of 8 to 10 reps as you build your strength and endurance.

Kettlebell Overhead Swing

- Hold a kettlebell by the horns.
- Squat, swinging the bell back between the legs.
- Using a hip thrust, swing the weight forward bringing it up and over the head.
- Swing the bell back down maintaining control and repeat in a fluid motion for 16 reps.

Kettlebell Figure 8

STEP 1   STEP 2   STEP 3   STEP 4

- Take the bell in your hand and stand with your feet spread to hip width. Lower your hips into a semi-squat, bringing the weight back between the legs.
- Grab the weight with the opposite hand and bring it back around the front as you stand.
- Return to the semi-squat and switch the weight to the other hand.

This is a terrific workout for the core!

One Arm Pull

- Hold a kettlebell in one hand with the other out to the side for balance, feet spread hip width apart.
- Squat while you maintain braced abs and a neutral back and then thrust your hips to stand.
- As you stand, the kettlebell should be drawn up to shoulder level with the elbow bent, holding the bell in front of the shoulder.
- Return to the starting position and repeat for a total of 8 to 10 reps.

Two Arm Pull

- Grip a kettlebell with both hands, standing with feet spread at hip width.
- Squat with your arms touching your inner thighs. Remember to push back with your butt and maintain a neutral back.
- As you use your hips and legs to stand, raise the kettlebell up, lifting your elbows up and above the shoulders keeping the bell close to your body.
- Return to the starting position, then complete a total of 8 to 10 reps.

Clean

- Begin as with the one arm pull, squat and stand using your hips for power.
- Bring the kettlebell straight up, rotating your elbow down as it reaches shoulder height.
- Bend your knees slightly to absorb the weight of the bell against your forearm. Keep the wrist neutral while maintaining a strong grip to control the bell.

Clean and Press

- Begin as with clean – squat and stand using your hips for power.
- Bring the kettlebell straight up, rotating your elbow down as it reaches shoulder height.
- Bend your knees slightly to absorb the weight of the bell against your forearm. Lift the kettlebell enough to avoid hitting your shoulder, because the bell will swing to the back of your hand from the front.
- From this position, press the bell straight up, over your head.
- Return the bell to the ground and start the movement for the next rep.

Kettlebell Snatch

- With your knees bent slightly and your feet shoulder width apart, use one hand to hold the bell between your knees.
- Squat slightly, then push off the ground with a jumping motion. Extend your knees and use your hips for power to bring the kettlebell up over your shoulder.
- Hold the kettlebell with the arm fully extended for one second and lower to the starting position. Repeat for a total of 8 to 10 reps and switch sides.

Russian Twist

- Hold a kettlebell with both hands either with the squeeze, by the horns, or by the handle, which is the most challenging. Feet should be shoulder width apart.
- With the kettlebell extended out from your waist and your elbows in tight to your sides, rotate to one side as far as you can comfortably with your abs braced, your lower body stable, and the hips square.
- Rotate to the opposite side controlling the momentum of the weight.

For a more intense workout, swing the kettlebell making sure you don't lose control or over-extend.

CHAPTER 8 – KETTLEBELL WORKOUT PROGRAMS

A kettlebell is an amazing piece of exercise equipment since it can be used by a beginner or advanced level athlete just as easily. There are, of course, different weights that make a difference in the difficulty of a workout and a variety of exercises that target particular muscle groups, but the basics are the same on the first day and for the first competition.

Virtually **all kettlebell workouts include exercises based on the same two moves – the lift and the swing**. From there, anyone can design a full-body workout that adds muscle, removes fat, provides explosive strength, and improves agility and balance. Workouts can be developed that provide excellent transfer of training for specific sports or activities, and kettlebell training even provides a rehabilitative program to relieve back pain.

Kettlebells provide a great workout for anyone, and programs can be designed to fit any specific needs.

There are *5 basic principles* that can be adjusted for any purpose:

- Choice of exercise
- Volume of exercise (reps and sets)
- Intensity of exercise
- Pattern (order) of exercises
- Length of rest intervals

For beginners or anyone not involved in regular exercise, it is important to check with a medical professional to determine whether kettlebell training or any new program is safe. Also, in spite of the wonderful DVDs and training literature that are available, it is best to find a gym or trainer where in-person instruction is given to be sure there are no problems with form that could result in injury.

Basic Workout

- **Warm up** with 2 sets each of 10 to 15 reps of the deadlift and waiter's walk:

  With the kettlebell in one hand raised above the head, lock out the elbow, maintain good posture and braced abs, and walk for 1 minute.

  Return to the rack position and switch hands.

- **Circuit exercises** are to be performed for 30 seconds alternating with 20 seconds of rest.

  Do all one-handed exercises on one side first, then switch sides to complete the next circuit for a total of 6 circuits (three with each hand):

  1. Two Hand Kettlebell Swing
  2. Clean and Press
  3. Reverse Lunge

- **Cool down** with some more simple stretches and a quick walk.

Simple Toning Workout

- Perform some stretches and a brief cardio **warm-up**.
- Beginning with a light weight, perform 10 reps of each exercise with only a 30-second rest between them. Perform 3 circuits, if possible, but do not sacrifice form to make the count!
    1. Clean and Press
    2. Kettlebell Two Arm Swing
    3. Two Arm Deadlift
    4. Windmill – Perform 5 with one hand, then switch for the remaining 5
- **Cool down** with controlled breathing, walking, and some stretches.

Easy to Modify Full-Body Workout

- Perform some simple **warm-up** activities to loosen your muscles and get your blood moving.
- Complete one circuit of 8 reps of each exercise with 30-second rest intervals 2 to 3 times a week. If this is comfortable, try to increase the workout to 10 reps for a few sessions, then 12 reps for another week. Return to 8 reps but perform 2 complete circuits and continue to add reps during the following weeks.

    1. Deadlift

        Begin with one weight, two hands. Or, one weight, one hand and do half the reps on each side. For more difficulty, use two weights with two hands.

    2. Swings

        Begin with one arm swings, half of the reps on each side. Or, do two arm swings and switch to alternating swings for more difficulty.

    3. Modified Turkish Get Up

        Switch to full get up for more difficulty.

    4. Kettlebell Pushups

        Remember, this is a more advanced move, especially with both hands resting on kettlebells. Be sure of your balance!

    5. Renegade Rows
    6. Front Lunge
    7. One Arm Press
    8. Halos

        Perform half of the reps in each direction.

- **Cool down** with some deep breathing and stretches.

The beauty of this workout is that you can begin slowly and easily and gradually add more reps, create slight variations to the moves, or perform both single- and two-handed moves to combine more isolated/more group muscle work.

By making some of these minor changes each week, you can keep going for many months with the same basic workout without needing to add weight for more of a challenge.

Kettlebell Workout for All-Over Strength

- ***Warm up*** with some stretches, jumping jacks, and/or a few deadlifts to get the blood flowing and muscles loosened.

- ***Circuit exercises*** are to be performed with high intensity and little (25 seconds) to no rest between different moves.
    1. Kettlebell Two-Handed Swings for 15 to 20 reps. [Switch to Figure 8s for more difficulty.]
    2. Pushups (with one – switch hands mid-way – or both hands on kettlebells) for 20 reps.
    3. Clean and Press for 10 to 12 reps each side.
    4. Lunge for 10 to 12 reps each leg.
    5. Russian Kettlebell Twist for 15 reps.

- ***Cool down*** with some deep breathing and stretches.

When this becomes 'easy,' add a few more reps to each exercise making sure you maintain proper form, posture, and breathing. For the next progression, drop back on the number of reps and try to complete 2 full circuits.

Killer Core Workout

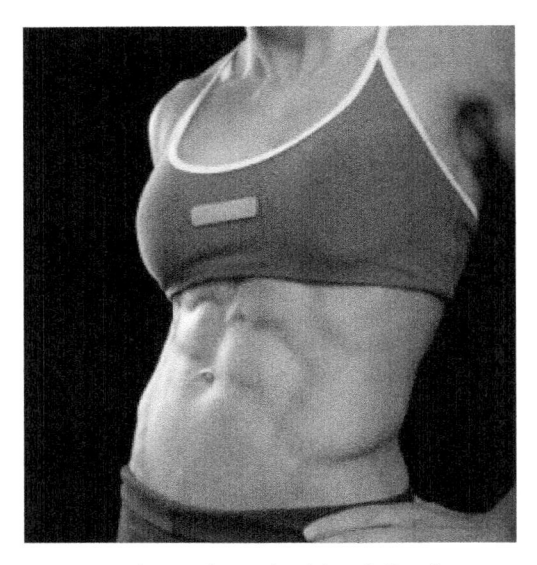

- **Warm up** your muscles and get the blood flowing.
- Perform each of the following exercises for 60 seconds with a 15-second interval between each.
    1. Reverse crunch – Holding a kettlebell firmly between both hands, straight up over your head, bring the kettlebell and your knees together in a classic crunch.

2. <u>Windmill</u>
3. <u>Russian Twist</u>
4. <u>Modified Turkish Get Up</u>
- ***Cool down*** with some deep breathing and stretches.

Beyond the Basics

The exercises included in these workouts are beginner and intermediate level, but most of them can be turned into advanced moves with plenty of practice. One way to **increase the level of difficulty of grinds** is to **hold the kettlebell a little further from the chest**. This calls for the firing of more muscles to maintain the hold. To make any workout tougher, **increase the reps and cut down the rest time between exercises**. Never work to exhaustion or to the point where you sacrifice form!

Once you have mastered one-handed and two-handed movements like the swing and progress to alternating hands, you are on your way to even more complex maneuvers such as tosses and juggles. Given the inherent safety issues with these moves, it is important to be perfectly comfortable with the basic moves and working on these advanced forms on the sand or grass wearing shoes, beginning with a lighter kettlebell than you normally work with.

Another factor to note with kettlebell training is that when you are ready to increase the weight for one exercise, it does not automatically mean you can for all. The most basic exercises can be ready for a weight increase well before more difficult or complex moves, and **it is always best to work on form and number of reps before moving to a higher weight**.

Muscle Building with Kettlebells

There is a lot of controversy about the role of kettlebell training in body building and hypertrophy. The dynamic nature of kettlebell exercises is more suited for toning muscles and, in many cases, does not lead to significant increases in strength. The general rule is that **heavier weights and few reps are used as a form of resistance training**, and **lighter kettlebells with more reps are used for** more of a **full-body cardio workout**.

That being said, however, kettlebell training is just one more tool in the bodybuilder's arsenal for achieving the greatest results. **Kettlebell workouts** provide a break from extreme weight sessions and **allow for the activation of a wider range of muscle groups leading to improved range of motion and more balanced musculature**. It has also been noted that developing correct kettlebell posture helps power lifters achieve more.

Kettlebell Workouts During Pregnancy

Pregnancy is not a good time to begin working out with kettlebells, but if you are used to weights and resistance training, there are some great kettlebell moves that can keep you in shape and help relieve stress. It is important to remember that some of the hormones created during pregnancy loosen the joints to prepare for the impending delivery so you need to use light(er) weights to avoid injuring those weight-bearing joints. During this time, it is especially important to discuss your fitness plans with your doctor.

Exercises that are considered safe during pregnancy include:

- Squats
- Swings
- Single leg deadlifts
- Alternating lunges
- Bent over rows
- Presses
- Farmer's walk

These moves are good to practice, even without the use of kettlebells, so you will be in top form, ready to add weight when the doctor clears you for exercise after delivery.

CHAPTER 9 – NUTRITION FOR WEIGHT LOSS AND MANAGEMENT

A fit and healthy body and your everyday needs require appropriate nutrition. That is a tremendous issue in today's fast-paced world, where convenience has turned our eating habits into a quick grab for something simple. Unfortunately, the general quality of the fast food we consume and the choices we make 'on the run' don't provide the best fuel to keep our bodies running at optimum efficiency.

What a Body Needs for a Healthy Diet

Many people take the wrong approach when they decide to 'diet.' The common misconception is lowering overall caloric intake, which usually involves cutting out carbohydrates. If those carbs come from junk food, cake, candy, and excess bread, then yes, removing them from the diet is an important step.

Unfortunately, maintaining a healthy diet that supports the energy needs of your body is not as simple as that. Drastic changes to the diet force the body to adapt its chemical processes, even if it is a switch to 'healthy foods.' When the body has to adapt, it relies on safeguarding its stores of glucose – especially in women – so what you are trying to eliminate becomes protected, making it – fat – much more difficult to lose.

The reason behind this effect is called 'homeostasis,' which is the body's way of maintaining chemical equilibrium. Every change you make creates a ripple effect that causes changes in other functions and processes. Just getting more activity and revving up the metabolism is a change to which your body reacts.

Don't get the idea that change is necessarily bad! Weight loss, better health, and a more efficient body are the result of change! The point is that you need to understand the connection between the changes you want to make and the overall effect on the body.

Turning the Body into a 'Fine-Tuned Machine'

Using an automobile as an analogy to the body, consider what using low-grade fuel and knock-off parts could do to an expensive race car. Imagine what would happen to performance if you used the wrong oil and poorly refined gasoline. If you are not eating the proper foods in the proper proportions, it is the same as cutting corners on the products you put in the engine of this car.

Taking the analogy a bit further, consider putting unbalanced tires on the car and removing some of the 'extra' parts that make the engine run smoothly and turn the wheels efficiently. You obviously would end up with a very bumpy ride, poor performance, and low gas mileage.

Compare these tires and parts to the nutritional elements you eat. Candy bars are no replacement for natural, raw foods! Your body will not work very efficiently or have sustained energy. If you are missing the right 'parts' – the appropriate nutritional building blocks – your performance and internal function will suffer.

If you demand high performance from your car or your body, the right fuel is necessary. Just like running out of gas in the car, your body will 'hit the wall' or suffer from complete fatigue if you rely on inadequate nutrition.

Carbohydrates Play a Crucial Role

Even though carbs have a bad reputation when it comes to discussing diet, they are actually extremely important for the generation of energy within the cells. **Eliminating carbs from the diet would be similar to not using oil in the engine**. The machine just will not work.

Carbohydrates are actually the source of the energy that fuels the function of your muscles. In purely nutritional terms, carbohydrates in the body are the elements that are broken down into smaller elements – sugars – that the cells use for immediate energy. These elements are stored in the muscles, liver, and in fat as glycogen for the body to access when it needs fuel.

This is the reason that sudden, significant changes in the diet can be counterproductive. If the body senses a drop in the supply of fuel, it works hard to protect them. What this means is that the metabolism actually slows down to preserve its energy! For women, this is particularly significant because the female body is designed to protect this available energy at all costs. That is why so many women are stuck in a cycle of yo-yo dieting, and it becomes more and more difficult to lose weight.

KETTLEBELL TRAINING

Before   After   After That

After Before   After   After After

Before Again   After Again   After After Again

If there is an extreme carbohydrate deficiency, and the glycogen stores are depleted, the body begins to metabolize its own protein for energy. This leads to the breakdown of hair, muscle, skin, and bone and results in the appearance that is associated with pictures of starving people. The kidneys are also forced to work harder to eliminate the waste products associated with protein synthesis and strong, unpleasant smelling urine is the result.

To sum up the ***importance of dietary carbohydrates***, not only do they supply the energy needed for cellular growth and function, they also perform these other functions within the body:

- Regulate blood sugar levels
- Provide nutrients for probiotics in the intestinal tract that promote proper digestion
- Aid in the absorption of calcium
- Assist in regulating blood pressure and controlling cholesterol levels
- Fuel the *CNS* (Central Nervous System) and the brain

Beyond Carbohydrates

Everybody is familiar with the idea of 'Daily Recommended Servings' and the 'Food Pyramid.' Unfortunately, many people ignore them! The human body requires a wide variety of nutrients from foods to grow, function, and remain healthy. **Selecting protein, vitamins, and minerals from natural sources and eliminating processed foods are two of the most important steps towards regaining and maintaining health**.

An appropriate diet consists of the following elements:

- Proteins from fish, fowl, lean meats, and nuts
- Vegetables and fruits
- Whole grains and alternate carbs such as barley, quinoa, flax, cornmeal, and beans
- Dairy including milk, cheese, and yogurt
- Healthy fats and oils (no trans fats!)
- Limited amounts of refined grains, potatoes, white rice (carbohydrates!)
- Only *minimal* amounts of other items such as salt, sugar, processed foods, and alcohol

Many people site allergies and other dietary restrictions as the reason they can't 'diet.' There is no ideal diet plan that will fit everyone's needs, so there are a few ***things to keep in mind when making dietary choices***. Common sense and a bit of knowledge regarding the ingredients and nutrients in foods go a long way in choosing the best nutritional elements.

1. Pay attention to **portion sizes** – Eat to live – don't live to eat! When you eat better foods, you will feel fuller and more satisfied.
2. Select a **wide range of food sources** to cover your nutritional requirements.
3. Make **smart carb choices** at each meal (starches and other high Glycemic Index carbs are preferable to sugars and other low GI carbs).
4. Choose **higher quality foods** – Less processed, more natural.
5. **Keep moving**! With better nutrition, you will have more energy and be more interested in staying physically active. This, in turn, enhances the body's ability to process the foods you eat more efficiently resulting in better health and fitness.
6. **Eat breakfast every day** – Enjoy quick, healthy snacks mid-morning and mid-afternoon.
7. **Include a small portion of lean protein** or high protein nuts with every meal and snack.
8. **Avoid caffeine** but drink green tea.
9. **Stay hydrated**! Never underestimate the importance of drinking plenty of water!
10. **Add spices and herbs** to help aid digestion, promote detoxification, and ease inflammation: *Anise, Basil, Burdock, Cilantro, Cinnamon, Cayenne, Cloves, Cumin, Garlic, Ginger, Ginseng, Licorice, Milk Thistle, Mint, Nutmeg, Oregano, Rosemary, Sage, Schizandra, Thyme, Turmeric.*

Maintain Adequate Hydration

When working out, especially for weight loss, keeping the body adequately hydrated is quite important since liquid lost through sweat needs to be replaced regularly. Most people don't drink enough water and even moderate workouts require a significant boost in intake. Intense workouts can create a demand of up to 2 to 3 gallons of water a day!

Water is important to the proper functioning of the body because it:

- Provides the fluid in the blood that transports oxygen and nutrients
- Flushes out toxins and cellular waste products
- Aids the digestive process and improves other body functions
- Helps to regulate body temperature

Detoxification is Not Just a Fad

Although there are many products on the market designed to detoxify the body, the truth of the matter is that it is relatively easy to do. The key is to maintain a healthy weight, eat a well-balanced diet, keep active, and drink plenty of water. Since toxins collect in body fat, **removing the fat is the best way to detoxify the body**.

The human body is amazingly efficient and utilizes many systems to promote the removal of toxins and wastes.

- Digestive tract
- Kidneys (to the bladder)
- Liver (to the blood stream)
- Lymphatic system
- Respiratory system and lungs
- Skin (through sweat)

When beginning a fat-burning regimen, you may actually feel tired, sore, and even nauseous at first because of the toxins that are released from the fat buildup in the blood stream. As these elements are filtered out and removed from the body, there will be an incredible improvement in your health, stamina, and even mental outlook. Along with dietary improvements and attention to adequate hydration, regular kettlebell workouts fine-tune the body's metabolism to function even more efficiently and improve overall cellular and systemic function.

CONCLUSION

Now that you have had a thorough look at the world of kettlebell training, you are probably ready to jump right in! With the information in this book, you have the basics for including kettlebell exercises in your workout routine and the resources for finding out more.

Kettlebelling is a fun, dynamic way to improve your overall fitness and assist in weight loss. Easy to do at home, in a gym, or at a professional training center, it is more than just one more exercise fad. Kettlebell workouts may not fulfill all your fitness needs, but for most people, they are plenty – resistance training and cardio all rolled into one session. For others, specific kettlebell exercises fill the gaps created when their workouts focus too intensely on activity-specific practice or limit the muscle groups that are addressed.

Please be sure to follow all the safety advice and precautions to avoid possible injury while working out with kettlebells. Remember that you need to start slowly with lighter weights until you perfect the basic moves. As you are ready to progress, practice new moves without weight to be sure you are using the proper form.

For an overall better toned body and weight maintenance, kettlebells offer a quick, enjoyable way to exercise, achieve your fitness goals, and have fun.

ABOUT THE AUTHOR

John Powers stumbled across kettlebell training at a young age. It was during his tenure as a quarterback on his high school football team that he realized he needed to get stronger and faster as quickly as possible. He started researching different workout methods and decided that he would try high intensity interval training (HIIT). This definitely revved up his speed and improved his throws. As he continued to study HIIT, he realized that it was the kettlebell workouts that were especially effective, and it was the kettlebells that he didn't mind using, even after a long day of school and practice.

As he continued studying, following his passion for personal training into college and beyond, kettlebell was the main tenant of his regimen. When he was the star of the grid iron, he used kettlebells to build real strength in his arms, making for more powerful throws. As he continued to pursue this form of training, he realized that kettlebells could be used to improve just about every aspect of his body, from his abs, to his legs, to his shoulders, to his back.

Kettlebells had the power to change his body, so he changed his mind about how they operate. He started learning as much as he could about the advantages of different weights and sizes and how they could be used to improve different muscles of the body. Then, once he had mastered the kettlebell exercises, he started bringing them to his clients. As a personal trainer, Powers has transformed hundreds of people's minds and bodies, opening their eyes to the power of the kettlebell.

Powers understands that the main problems people have with working out on a regular basis is that it is too boring, too time consuming, or that their bodies too quickly become accustomed to the workouts, and they are no longer effective. Kettlebells are a solution to all of those problems, and that is why he has written this book. With kettlebells as the focus of his own training and the training he teaches to his clients, he knows how fun and efficient these workouts can be. Along with his love of HIIT, kettlebells are his passion, and he knows how to help you build a workout that will be fun and effective.

Printed in Dunstable, United Kingdom